Building Children's Resilience

One building block at a time

Essential tips for parents of children birth-12

by Maggie Dent

Pennington Publications
PO Box 312, Murwillumbah, NSW 2484
Website: www.maggiedent.com

Title: Building Children's Resilience: One building block at a time
Edition: First
Author: Dent, Maggie.

Date of Publication: 29 February 2016.

Based on the book *Real Kids in an Unreal World: Building Resilience and Self Esteem in Today's Children* by Maggie Dent (2008)

ISBN: 978-0-9758456-9-1

Layout and Design: Katharine Middleton, Ink Box Graphics
Back cover image: Samara Wheeldon Photography

10 Resilience BUILDING BLOCKS
for children aged 0 – 12 years

I pay my deepest respect to the traditional custodians of the land where I was born and raised—The Noongar peoples of Western Australia. And I also pay my respects to Aboriginal peoples and Torres Strait Islanders, past and present, who have also walked and cared for this land for over 40,000 years. May we all find ways to walk gently and compassionately on these ancient lands and come to a place where all children born have a sense of belonging deeply.

Contents

What is RESILIENCE?

Today's world is very different to the world that many parents were raised in. Some of us still remember living without TV, computers, hand-held devices and smart phones. Yet the advances and increasing knowledge of modern society are not producing more resilient children or young people.

Resilience refers to the ability to successfully manage life, and adapt to change and stressful events in healthy and constructive ways. It is about the capacity to bounce back from positive and negative life experiences. To develop emotional and psychological buoyancy in childhood gives children a better prospect of being able to thrive as adults rather than just survive.

> "A universal capacity which allows a person, group or community to prevent, minimize or overcome the damaging effects of adversity."
>
> — The International Resilience Project (2005).

Dr James Neill from the University of Canberra in Australia says:

"In humanistic psychology resilience refers to 'an individual's ability to thrive and fulfil potential despite or perhaps because of stressors or risk factors'".

At an international resilience conference in Canada in 2015 the perspective of what resilience is had changed somewhat to it being a capacity to thrive that is determined by the systems and environments that surround an individual or community. Essentially our ability to overcome significant adversity can only become a reality when we can access people and resources that can help us.

Many of our children and teenagers are facing emotional, social and mental problems and disorders. They may also face issues like struggling with stress, obesity, poor body image, low self-esteem and self-worth, stress and disconnection.

The early years starting from conception are important in helping our children to be better equipped to live in today's world of constant change. Research shows that physical, intellectual, emotional and social development is rapid during this time. Most of the important developments are invisible and difficult to measure, and often the little things are the big things. It all impacts on a child's ability to be resilient later in life. Modern life has created an environment where intensive parenting has become more of the norm and, while protecting our children is a parent's prime responsibility, over protecting them from the normal bumps and bruises that occur in childhood may be contributing to the weakening of resilience in today's children.

Children need to experience disappointment, challenge, failure and boundaries to fully develop the interpersonal and personal skills that allow people to live in society. They also need to have a voice, and age-dependent moments of autonomy where they get to have a sense of control over their life. However, too much autonomy will lead to overindulgent, permissive and unpleasantly challenging (possibly narcissistic) behaviour that will create conflict and distress. As parents, we need to find a balance.

Over the past 30 years we seem to have become more focused on the possible deficits or problems that can occur rather than on the strengths that exist within every child. In many countries, such as the UK, US, Canada and Australia schooling systems are much more test-driven and this seems to have pushed a 'hurry up' approach to the early years of life. Our young children are sometimes being seen as sources of data rather than as unique miracles—all different, all developing at different rates with individual strengths and challenges. This apparent homogenising of children before they get to school is stealing time from childhood that used to be used to develop social and emotional competence. We're stealing their freedom to explore and be adventuresome through play and this has created stressors that are impacting young children deeply. In turn this shift has created less resilience in both our children and teens.

Childhood is a journey and there is no perfect world, perfect parent or correct way to raise a child. There is no perfect child. Families today live in a world of massive change and uncertainty. In many ways, parenting is now more confusing than it has ever been because of the massive availability of information, together with the invisible and overt pressures of consumerism that have saturated the parenting world. However, real kids can thrive in our unreal and often chaotic world.

This pocket book outlines 10 key building blocks for children birth–12 years of age that can help build healthy self-esteem and strengthen their resilience. These building blocks show the different areas that a parent, school or community can focus on in order to build resilience for life. Any one building block will help, and the more the better.

This holistic model was drawn from modern research and the ancient wisdom of indigenous cultures around the world. Interestingly enough, these building blocks will work in any culture, in any country and with any child. Resilience can be built in families with limited financial resources as well as within remote rural communities that are often scattered a long way from major cities. This is a strength-focused, common-sense model that resonates with early years' educators, parenting educators, families and schools. Not all of our children are going to be academically gifted or competent, however if they are capable and resilient, they will navigate this strange journey called life in a way that will allow them to thrive and create a life of worth and meaning.

> "The strongest oak of the forest is not the one that is protected from the storm and hidden from the sun. It's the one that stands in the open where it is compelled to struggle for its existence against the winds and rains and the scorching sun."
>
> — Napoleon Hill (1883-1970)

Building BLOCK 1

Positive, healthy pregnancy

The first step in building healthy, resilient children is for mothers to have as healthy a pregnancy as possible with loving support, excellent nutrition, and an absence of alcohol and medically unauthorised drugs.

Research shows that a foetus is responsive to the mother's changing emotional state through hormones passed through the placenta. Stressful and traumatic experiences in the womb and throughout the early months of life are registered in the brain as 'emotional memory', and help to shape the forming psyche and personality of a child (Grille, 2013).

> "Behavioural disturbances as serious as delinquency, schizophrenia, ADHD, depression and substance abuse have been associated with highly stressful experiences in the womb; such as severe marital discord, or maternal hostility or rejection towards the foetus."
>
> — Robin Grille, *Parenting for a Peaceful World* (2013).

Avoiding alcohol will assist the development of a baby's healthy brain. Research has now proven that any alcohol consumption during pregnancy can damage a baby's brain and impedes early development on all levels. This creates a challenge for developing life resilience as it can affect a child's IQ, physical growth and even cause social and behavioural problems. The safest thing to do to ensure your baby is not affected is not to drink at all during your pregnancy.

Healthy food, physical activity and supplementation—especially of folic acid and iron—provide the expectant mother with the best chance of delivering a healthy baby. Some foods are not recommended during pregnancy and it is up to the doctor or midwife attending the expectant mother to provide her with this information. Smoking is one of the things to avoid, both during pregnancy and when around children. Genetic defects, abuse of any kind, brain injuries and bad environments immediately after birth (post partum) can contribute to an unhealthy brain and poor baby development.

Physical and emotional abuse of the mother will also cause stress to both mother and baby. We can help those we love by creating support networks and providing caring respite.

Creating a supportive sisterhood

In many cultures, it is common to see the whole family taking responsibility for raising a child and assisting the mother. This includes help from older siblings, extended family and other community members.

In our modern society many mothers-to-be live a long way from their families and creating a healthy 'sisterhood'—a circle of women who are also having families—is incredibly helpful in this early stage of the parenting journey. If you know someone who is expecting a baby be mindful of what you say and do, and offer compassionate support in any way you can. If you are expecting a child, make sure you seek out a safe community of support—whether that be through mothers' groups, antenatal classes, online parent support groups, or introducing yourself to other mums in your neighbourhood.

Parent tips for a healthy pregnancy

- ☑ A healthy pregnancy is the best start for a healthy baby.
- ☑ It is best to completely avoid alcohol, drugs and smoking while pregnant.
- ☑ Healthy food, exercise and supplements (especially folic acid and iron) can support you to have a healthy pregnancy and baby.
- ☑ Stress can impact a baby in the womb so try to manage your own stress during pregnancy and ask for help if you need it.
- ☑ Babies can be born with emotional memory.
- ☑ Know that a healthy birth is not always a given—there are risks that can occur at any time.
- ☑ Ensure you are monitored by a health professional throughout pregnancy.
- ☑ Try to find a support network who will be there for you during your pregnancy and once you become a mother.
- ☑ Everyone in our community needs to support pregnant women regardless of age, culture or social status.

Building BLOCK 2

Good nutrition

It is essential that babies have their nutritional and safety needs met first and foremost. Primary carers need to make this a priority, because babies and toddlers are completely dependent on them for their food and drink.

During pregnancy and the first two years of a child's life, the need for adequate, healthy nutrition is critical. Recent studies in brain research show that good nutrition not only allows healthy physical growth to occur it also supports neuron development, and improves mood and behaviour. The brain almost doubles in size in the first two years of life, so it is important to provide your baby with good nutrition.

> “ Learning restraint around the treats of life helps build a less self-indulgent attitude to foods that should be eaten in moderation. Young children are often unable to make good health decisions themselves, and early indulgence in the wrong foods can lead to obesity.

Nutrition has become a very hot topic in our modern world—thanks to the Internet we receive endless, often contradictory, information about what is good and bad for us. There are food fads and diets that come and go, many of which are often unsustainable, unrealistic and not based on science. Food that is closest to nature, and as unprocessed as possible, is recommended for both children and adults. Food that is grown in alignment with the seasons is the very best food for you. It is created with the highest vibration energetically and is meant to be eaten fresh, not 12 months later when it comes out of cold storage.

A balanced approach to children's food patterns is recommended. Aiming for an 80:20 ratio where 80% of the time your children are eating healthy, nutrient dense, unprocessed foods and allowing 20% of the time to enjoy the things that are less healthy, however often incredibly delicious. The 80% is healthy, everyday food and the 20% should be seen as treats or special occasion foods.

Hidden nasties

In some places such as Denmark, Sweden, New York and California, trans fatty acids have been banned in food for children under 5 and this is partly because there is research to show excessive consumption of trans fats can impede brain development. In Australia, the UK and many other countries there is no such protection. Trans fats are found in almost all commercially produced foods—cakes, doughnuts, biscuits, muesli slices, pizzas, pies, pastries, burgers and potato crisps and the like. Keeping the consumption of these products to less than 20% of a child's diet is protecting them from unwanted harm.

Additives and colourings are also of great concern in how they may affect our children's lives. Many additives cause adverse reactions such as allergies, asthma, hyperactivity and rashes. If your child's behaviour or health is concerning you, being mindful of what 'numbers' are in their food might help.

Some of the dangerous designated numbers to avoid in foods are: 102, 4R, 124, 110, 122, 104, 129 and 211.

Different countries use different numbers and food safety standards vary around the world. Also, new additives are being developed all the time so it's a good idea to stay up-to-date with the various research into the effects of additives and colours. One good site in Australia is www.additivealert.com.au

Excessive sugar consumption, especially in fruit juice, soft drinks and lollies/candy (but also in many 'healthy' low fat foods found in the health food aisle) can have a negative effect on children's moods and behaviour as well as cause other health concerns. As sugar is now hidden in many foods, especially many cereals that are recommended for children, it is not always the obvious consumption that is the problem. Again, check the labels when you're shopping to do a comparison of the best options for your family. The same goes for excessive salt hidden in food—check the sodium levels before you buy.

> “ Studies on obesity show that being overweight is more the result of poor quality, nutritionally depleted foods eaten in large quantities than a lack of exercise. This is something that can be easily changed.

Food for the soul

Food is about so much more than getting your nutritional needs met. Humans have always gathered together around food and it has a fundamentally important role at building bondedness and a sense of belonging in families. Sharing food around a table or a fire is an ancient way of creating human connectedness, which builds memories that last for life.

Many of us are triggered by smells from certain foods that take us back to a memory of our childhood. Memories that are built around pleasurable moments in life—especially ones that are repeated, like bush barbecues, Christmas celebrations and birthday parties—are linked via our smell, visual and gustatory memories. Research shows that we have a positive endorphin response to the smell of wholesome food that was prepared often by someone we love.

Maybe it's the secret ingredient that is put into food that is prepared for us by someone we love. Making memories with food is important and having healthy, positive rituals around sharing food can strengthen a child's sense of belonging especially in times of conflict or trauma.

Remember you buy the food that goes into your pantry. Children will almost always choose food high in sugar and fat as it releases the neurotransmitter serotonin, which is a feel-good brain chemical. If there is only healthy, wholesome food in your pantry and refrigerator, your children will make a healthy choice.

Top tips for nutrition for babies, toddlers and children

- ☑ Begin with breast milk if possible for the first six months at least (remember sometimes successful breastfeeding requires support so don't be afraid to ask for help).
- ☑ Water is the best fluid for babies and toddlers, other than breast milk or formula.
- ☑ Ensure sufficient protein for growing babies and toddlers.
- ☑ No soft drinks until at least five years of age, and only then in very limited amounts if at all.
- ☑ Avoid cordials and fruit juice.
- ☑ Choose only pure fruit juice and mix with water. Never put sweet drinks, including sweet milk drinks or juice, into babies' bottles.

- ☑ Avoid deep fried foods including fast foods like hamburgers, hot dogs and chips.
- ☑ Avoid potato chips, crisps and similar snacks.
- ☑ Avoid pre-packaged doughnuts, cakes, biscuits and pastries.
- ☑ Avoid unhealthy cereals low in fibre, and high in sugar and salt.
- ☑ Avoid any foods with MSG (monosodium glutamate).
- ☑ Choose whole fruits.
- ☑ Choose wholegrain breads with fresh salads and lean meat, chicken, egg or cheese.
- ☑ Choose preservative-free bread.
- ☑ Allow young children to 'graze' on healthy foods, rather than eat to adult time schedules.
- ☑ Avoid telling children to clean their plate.
- ☑ Avoid making children eat when they are not hungry.
- ☑ Ensure children eat foods that provide essential fatty acids such as Omega 3. Foods that contain this include oily fish, linseed, sunflower seeds and walnuts (don't introduce nuts too early as they may be a choking/ allergy hazard... may be OK after six months as a paste providing allergy is not an issue).
- ☑ Vitamin and mineral supplements (known as micronutrients) can be beneficial while children are growing—especially iodine, iron, zinc and vitamin B12.
- ☑ Ensure children eat a breakfast that contains protein. The brain needs it to function properly.
- ☑ Avoid sugary products, drinks and sweets in packed lunches.
- ☑ Keep lollies, chocolates and sweets to a minimum.
- ☑ Keep portion sizes moderate, regardless of age.
- ☑ Avoid negative environmental factors such as cigarette smoke, polluted air, mites, moulds and allergens, poisonous minerals like lead and mercury (found in some fish, shark and mussels; dental amalgam; some medications; and pesticides and fungicides), and excessive electro-radiation (microwave ovens, mobile phones and overhead heavy duty power lines).

Building BLOCK 3

Safe, nurturing care within the circle of family

I once heard a paediatric specialist say he believes the number-one important factor in parenting babies and toddlers is that you need to spend a lot of time with at least one person "who is completely nuts about you!"

Belonging is another way of explaining attachment, which is the relationship between a key adult and a child, and then their wider community. Babies, toddlers and children need to have 'big people' they can trust to nurture and care for them. These people help guide and teach them all that they will need to know in life so they can become independent, capable adults who will hopefully in many cases find mates, breed and ensure the survival of the species.

> "A secure attachment happens when parents are able to be sensitive to their child's cues, responsive to his needs and treat him lovingly. This pays instant dividends in both child development and also in behaviour."
>
> — Jo Jackson King, *Raising the Best Possible Child* (2010).

Attachment is the 'super glue' that holds a child in close **proximity** to a parent/caregiver. A child is meant to pursue proximity, which means being close to their big person so that they feel safe and are safe. Attachment is as important to healthy child development as eating or sleeping. Indeed, in much of the most recent research, strong attachment and bondedness can be shown to be the most significant influence on emotional wellbeing, mental health and physical health for life.

> "You are teaching one of the few human beings who will be entirely entrusted to you, how to laugh, learn and love people. There is nothing more worthwhile that you will ever do."
>
> — Steve and Shaaron Biddulph, *Love, Laughter and Parenting* (2001).

'Primary attachments' are the big people of central importance in a child's life—typically parents. It is helpful for parents of babies and toddlers to have a circle of caring adults who can share the raising of children. This allows for support, guidance and respite, which helps every parent, especially tired mummies, cope with this intensive time of life. For children who are in long-day child care, the early years' educators who form a loving, caring connection to a young child are technically a source of primary attachment, often called 'secondary attachment' figures.

A playful, supportive community

Family, friends or community support networks like playgroups, walking groups or people you may gather with for regular outings, are beneficial in the first years of a baby's life because they offer additional interaction and respite. Parents will not always be able to meet every social need of their growing baby. Exhausted parents are less likely to have energy to play games or interact with a toddler, so they often need support to make sure they can support this need in their children. Also, games and activities build pathways to a child's abilities for learning basic literacy later in school (and so much more as you will read about in the next Building Block).

> "Keeping the natural world out of the reach of children seems to be our national passion. In fact greater numbers of children are brought up in the artificial world of cement, asphalt, plastics and the virtual reality of television while fewer each year experience a world of nature and the unfolding of organic life."
>
> —Joseph Chilton Pearce, *The Biology of Transcendence* (2004).

I totally salute this view and urge parents, grandparents and carers to allow children to explore the natural world with the vim and vigour that is encoded in their genes. Allow children to experience the exquisite moments of joy when jumping in puddles, diving into piles of Autumn leaves, feeding (with appropriate wild feed) ducks in a local lake, catching tadpoles and making mud pies as only children can. These are the experiences that

children are meant to have so that they can better cope with the adult world of responsibility and stress when it does arrive.

A safe circle of support and care provides simple connections between a carer and their baby, toddler or child. Fathers are vitally important in this circle and may need to be encouraged when they are first-time fathers. Simple activities like reading favourite picture books, reciting nursery rhymes, and playing hand and clapping games all build fun and smart brains. Real experiences are trips to the beach or the park, helping in the garden with grandad, helping nanna bake biscuits, and feeding the chooks. The child learns how to be useful. Given the chance to explore their mildly stimulating world within the protective safety of people who care about them, children develop emotional, social and spiritual competence. These competencies stay with them for life.

Reading to children

Some vital things happen when children are read to yet these may go unnoticed by adults. Reading books to your young children every day can help them:

- develop a love of books and reading
- develop imagination, creativity and exploration skills
- strengthen brain pathways and memory, enhance brain development and recall of language
- develop an understanding of text, and the meaning and mechanics of language
- develop vocabulary and comprehension
- enhance their curiosity
- stimulate themselves in multi-sensory ways
- form a bond with a caring adult
- enjoy a calming activity that is largely still
- build a strong foundation so that they can become successful readers for life.

Paediatrician Dr Emmi Pikler and her key advocates, especially Magda Gerber, believe that the following principles apply to raising and caring for infants and toddlers.

10 principles based on a philosophy of respect

1. Involve infants and toddlers in things that concern them.
2. Invest in quality time, when you are totally available to individual infants and toddlers.
3. Learn each child's unique ways of communicating and also teach yours—don't underestimate children's ability to communicate even though their verbal language skills may be non-existent or minimal.
4. Invest time and energy to build a total person—concentrate on the whole child.
5. Respect infants and toddlers as worthy people. Don't treat them as objects or cute little empty headed people to be manipulated.
6. Be honest with your feelings.
7. Model the behaviour you want to teach.
8. Recognise problems as learning opportunities and let infants and toddlers try to solve their own problems. Don't rescue them, constantly make life easy for them or protect them from all problems.
9. Build security by building trust. Don't teach distrust by being undependable or frequently inconsistent.
10. Be concerned about the quality of development in each stage. Don't rush infants and toddlers to reach developmental milestones.

– Source: from Magda Gerber, *The RIE Manual for Parents and Professionals* (1979) quoted in Janet Gonzalez-Mena and Dianne Widmeyer Eyer, *Infants, Toddlers and Caregivers* (2007).

The key points of this approach are:

Respectful-Responsive-Reciprocal-Interaction

This approach (RIE parenting) encompasses the whole child rather than a sum of a number of parts. It also acknowledges that all children are unique—some children develop faster in certain areas, while in other areas they may be delayed. This is not seen as a problem, merely a reflection on the unique journey of a toddler or child. The authors of the principles have a clear expectation that with quality care, which is responsive and respectful of each individual child, they will grow on all levels. This approach does not have a prescribed list of targets that children should meet at certain ages; it simply honours children to grow and develop in alignment with their innate pathways while being surrounded by caring, aware adults.

It is important that parents and carers of children resist the hurried world we now live in. Nature has provided the means to support babies to become healthy children for over five million years without needing to hurry them. There is a serious danger that 'kid-pushing' can be very detrimental to a child's growth, especially psychologically and if he or she develops a premature sense of failure or "I am dumb".

> "Children who are over scheduled into weekly activities may inadvertently be learning that life is about having every moment of their lives filled with entertainment and prescribed activities. Consequently, opportunities to show initiative, play alone and/or create experiences for themselves appear to have become lost."
>
> — Kathy Walker, *What's The Hurry: Reclaiming Childhood in an Overscheduled World* (2005).

We must never forget that child development cannot be hurried, no matter how inconvenient that may be for the adults of our 'hurry up' world. Each child has a built-in timetable that dictates just when s/he will crawl, sit up and start to walk. Given a safe environment, their development flows naturally. A key aspect to remember is that a child's important learning milestones and developmental growth come **when the baby is ready, not when the adult decides it is time**.

Of course, if ever you have a strong feeling that your child is significantly not meeting a developmental milestone that would normally be expected of them at a certain age, don't hesitate to seek advice from your paediatrician, child health nurse, doctor, allied health practitioner or other professional. Many developmental issues can be helped with early intervention. Follow your gut and ask questions.

The overstimulation of modern childhood

Babies need repeated experiences in which they can self-direct and build the neural connections that create memory. *When children are bored they are wired to move on to something else, to continue to engage their inquisitive brains.* Learning how to manage boredom is a vital stage of development that over-stimulated babies and children need to master. When adults over-direct an infant's learning, with noisy toys, screens and even educational DVDs, games or apps, they run a serious risk of invalidating the baby's natural curiosity and also causing hidden stress. Activities that use gross motor skills, like learning to catch a large soft ball, are fun to do with a small child and are so important in terms of hand-eye coordination. Early over-stimulation causes the baby's brain to flood with stress hormones, which can cause them to be distressed and it can hard wire them to be overly sensitive to stress for the rest of their lives. So it's important to relax, sit on the couch or grass and simply watch your baby or toddler interact with the real world through the magic of movement in their own time and in their own way.

Keep in mind childhood is not a race—go slow and appreciate every single stage of your child's life. Try not to wish away any stage in preference for the next one because every stage has gifts and challenges. Children learn by doing and they will be noisy, untidy, messy and unpredictable. This is normal and at times parenting can be tiring, exhausting and frustrating. This too is normal.

You—the parent—are the most important teacher your child will ever have and being able to do that while loving them unconditionally is going to challenge you most days. However every teachable moment that you have matters.

Keep in mind:

> "90% of children's inappropriate behaviour is developmentally appropriate because they are children." — Dr Gordon Neufeld (2005)

Recommendations for yourself and the care of very young children

- ☑ **Become informed about babyhood and early childhood before becoming pregnant.**
- ☑ **Take care of your physical and emotional needs during pregnancy.**
- ☑ **Create as much time as possible to devote to mothering and caring for your newborn.**
- ☑ **Create a supportive network before your baby arrives.**
- ☑ **Become securely attuned to your baby's needs.**
- ☑ **Avoid child care outside the home for as long as possible.**
- ☑ **Be aware that toddlers under two years of age may not be able to socialise easily.**

- ☑ Avoid using the TV or any other screens as a babysitter, particularly under two.
- ☑ Avoid too many toys.
- ☑ Avoid too much talking and coaching.
- ☑ Be aware of the possible long-term effects of extensive child care—more than 30 hours per week in babies and toddlers under three can cause problem behaviours, especially those associated with anxiety, aggression and oppositional behaviour. See if you and/or your partner can manage to work part-time in the very early years and perhaps seek family help some of the time.
- ☑ Committed parents sharing child care of young children in their own home is preferable to outside child care of babies and toddlers under two years of age, however obviously this is not an economic possibility for many so choose your care wisely.
- ☑ When choosing carers of your child keep in mind the importance of providing loving, consistent care—safe, gentle touch, soothing words, capacity to reassure and time to do so.
- ☑ Become informed about the key issues in outside child care. Enquire about ratios of staff to children, how staff manage challenging behaviours, fussy eaters and anxious children. Check on the staff turnover.
- ☑ Help build a relationship between your child and their carers... talk about them, have a photo of them on the fridge, communicate with carers about your child's day and any changes in their world.
- ☑ Family day care where there is one primary carer and a small number of children in a home often works better for our sensitive children.
- ☑ Trained nannies in the home who meet the above concerns, and who become a part of the family network, can offer a positive alternative to outside child care for some people.
- ☑ Finding what works best for each of your children may involve exploring many options and what works for one may not work for another.

Building BLOCK 4

Plenty of play

> "If we love our children and want them to thrive, we must allow them more time and opportunity to play, not less. Yet policymakers and powerful philanthropists are continuing to push us in the opposite direction—toward more schooling, more testing, more adult direction of children, and less opportunity for free play."
>
> —Dr Peter Gray, *"The play deficit"*, Aeon (18 September 2013).

One of the saddest things in the raising of children today has been the disrespect and invalidation of the importance of play. In the early years especially, play-based learning has lost its value and been replaced by formalised learning that requires sitting still at a desk.

What is stopping our children from being more active and playing more?

According to Australian academics Joanne Landy and Alice Brown, the authors of an excellent resource for educators and the carers of children called *Kids With More Zip* (2008), there appears to be a number of variables associated with today's childhood inactivity.

- An increase in screen-based activity and labour saving devices
- Child safety concerns that impact on children playing in the streets, local parks and walking or cycling to school
- A decrease in play environments and play opportunities
- Issues of modern living such as more parents working, less recreation time and an overuse of cars.

— Landy and Brown (2008)

As I wrote in my latest book, *9 Things: A back-to-basics guide to calm, common-sense, connected parenting Birth-8* (2014):

> Play is the way babies and children develop their sense of self, sense of the world, and sense of where they fit in. Children are biologically wired to play. Play is very serious business for them. Opportunities for play are essential because they help a child learn many of the emotional and social competencies. These cannot be developed through direct verbal interaction with adults. Solo play, parallel play, imaginative, adult-directed and interactive play are all healthy forms of play for children to experience in childhood. However, there are so many factors that are eroding children's opportunities to play and so many busy parents tell me they simply struggle to make the time for such opportunities. Time is such a precious thing in our chaotic and busy world and so often creating the time to allow children to play freely, autonomously and with gay abandon is now a rare occurrence.

> "Having sufficient time to play is important—big blocks of time without being disturbed and made to hurry is important for children and adults. We need time to chill out, relax, to let our ideas flow, have conversations with real or imaginary friends, to test our ideas and theories and replay, retest and rethink them."
>
> — Neville Dwyer, *Being Adventurous* (2013).

Play is a much underrated but incredibly vital part of children's development. Put simply, "play grows the brain". As Hara Estroff Marano highlighted in her book, *A Nation of Wimps* (2008), play helps to grow the parts of our brains that control how we retain information, regulate our emotions and manage our behaviour. She writes of the cleverness of nature in giving us something that is not goal directed (play) to "create the mental machinery for being goal directed".

Important brain development is happening while a child is playing. Some brain development requires tumbling, spinning, balancing and rolling because it develops the sensory system. These activities help develop the cerebellum. Some studies have linked dyslexia and ADHD with under-developed cerebellums.

From around two years of age, toddlers are capable of learning social skills that will strengthen their life-coping skills. They are starting to develop their sense of 'self' and need for autonomy and personal independence. The stronger a person's sense of identity and independence, and the life skills that support these attributes, the better their resilience.

The parts of the brain concerned with regulating emotion and attitudes to human relations require human contact to develop. Only real interactions build emotional competencies—not watching it on a screen. Socialising is an excellent way for toddlers to achieve this development and Australian child psychologist Dr Louise Porter believes that children are often unable to socialise well until they are around three years of age. Self-initiated play is often better than rigidly organised activities with adult intervention, even if they may seem beneficial to cognitive development. Children have an enormous curiosity and thirst for life when exploring their world, especially with other children. Curiosity and innovative, flexible thinking are attributes of resilient people.

Playing verbal games with a child from the early years ensures the development of verbal and processing skills around visual and auditory cues that will help them learn to read. These activities also help children to manage their impulses, learn about persistence, and about winning and losing. Card games, Connect and pick-up-sticks help develop hand/eye coordination, memory and concentration. Children also need to understand it is OK to make mistakes sometimes, and parents need to understand that it is OK for their children to make mistakes too.

Singing and counting games for young children help stimulate their brains to develop patterning and sequencing strategies that help with cognitive processing later in life. These are very important in developing the resilience pathways.

Keep in mind that children are developing by interacting with the world through experiencing it via their five senses, and all five senses need to be utilised. An overuse of screens can delay sensory development in other areas and this is why keeping a balance of activities helps both in the early years and in the primary school years.

Toys, play and creativity

An important message to remember about children and play is that you do not need to spend a lot of money buying toys. There is some research that suggests too many toys and too much TV are two of the reasons why our children are struggling with concentration and attentiveness in our classrooms.

One of the things that our modern world cannot measure is our capacity for creative thought. This is something that children normally do really well and it is linked to the 'seeking mechanism', which is very active in children's brains. When we give them toys that work one way we can often stunt their natural curiosity. Imaginary play is incredibly powerful on so many levels for children. Without a healthy mechanism for seeking the capacity to problem-solve creatively we can struggle later in life when adversity comes visiting. How do you rebuild your home after a natural disaster or rebuild your life after the loss of your partner without the capacity for creative thinking and problem solving? Resilient people have this capacity and it can be nurtured in childhood.

> "One of the great tragedies for children, however is that our society has forgotten how much imaginative play contributes to the skills that lead to life success. Why? I think it is because imaginative play doesn't have a 'product' that can be used as 'evidence of learning' and time well spent."
>
> — Jo Jackson King, *Raising the Best Possible Child* (2010).

Some of the best play can occur using simple things like cardboard boxes, buckets, ice cream containers and empty plastic bottles. What a great way to recycle and provide play opportunities for young children.

Imaginative play creates creative minds that see the world differently, problem-solve innovatively and bring an incredible richness into human life. As Cambridge University psychology and education researcher Dr David Whitebread (2012) writes in his report *The Importance of Play*:

> "You can't teach creativity; all you can do is let it blossom. Little children, before they start school, are naturally creative. Our greatest innovators, the ones we call geniuses, are those who somehow retain that childhood capacity, and build on it, right through adulthood."
>
> — Whitebread, et al. (2012)

Play researcher Tim Gill explores play by looking at the long-lasting effects in the United Kingdom of removing risk from childhood.

> "Activities and experiences that previous generations enjoyed without a second thought have been labelled as troubling or dangerous, while adults who still permit them are branded as irresponsible ... society appears to have become unable to cope with any adverse outcomes whatsoever, no matter how trivial or improbable."
>
> —Tim Gill, *No Fear* (2007).

Children need opportunities for creative, exploratory play in stress-free environments with time and freedom. Thankfully schools and communities are now embracing a less risk-averse approach to children's play. More and more research is showing that the modern, supposedly safe, playgrounds are diminishing our children's capacity to assess and manage risk. There are enormous benefits to allowing children to experience the bumps and bruises that can occur while at play. Instead of hovering over our children, we must challenge the perception of 'good enough parenting' and allow our children to make choices and experience the occasional setback and disappointment.

Even though over protection comes from a place of love it is diminishing and disrespecting our children's capacity to learn how to deal with life when it lets us down or we feel disappointed or unhappy. We need to allow children to experience disappointment before they start school. A great way to start would be to change the rules of 'pass the parcel' back to its original game plan. There is supposed to be only one winner so that we are able to coach and encourage our children to deal with losing or not getting what we want. We need to validate to them that losing 'sucks' and it doesn't feel very good. However there are always more games and more chances of winning.

The return to nature play

Anecdotal evidence shows that many preschools and primary schools are returning to planning for longer times for children to play outside in natural environments with dirt, trees, water and green grass. They are noticing an increase in creative play, social cohesion, better problem solving, negotiation skills and immersion in the play experience. Children are calmer, happier, less anxious and less stressed. Cognitive learning is still taking place with unstructured play. This play is vital to developing social skills like sharing, taking turns, communication skills, dealing with disappointment and delayed gratification.

> “Tim Gill writes of how children of previous generations learned to take care and manage risks, because they knew that playgrounds were potentially dangerous. Today, children believe that playgrounds are safe and so they take little care and do not learn healthy risk assessment or management. This is commonly known as ‘risk compensation’. It is worth asking however, “What are we risking with our children if they are never exposed to risk?” There will always be some benefits as well as some concerns when exploring the question of risk in childhood. Technically our world is safer today than it has ever been, and many of our fears are irrational and fed by the media and the insurance industry.”
>
> — Maggie Dent, *9 Things* (2014).

The return of nature playgrounds in schools and communities across Australia is giving children opportunities to engage far more deeply in play activities that they can change and rearrange. This gives them a strong sense of confidence in their own autonomy and is also a great way to build self-regulation and concentration. When children are able to conquer something that makes them stretch and grow, that makes them aim, persist, practise and strive, we are building resilience on all levels.

Physical activity reduces the likelihood of obesity, and it is also important for the functioning of the brain. It supports learning and memory function, and also the repair and maintenance of neural circuits. Physical activity has also been shown to reduce stress and aggression, and it helps regulate mood by increasing the release of serotonin and dopamine—essential for emotional and cognitive wellbeing. Being physically active may also be a protective factor against depression (Jensen, 2006).

Play is the best way to develop a healthy enjoyment of physical activity, and it should always be fun to help build a positive attitude to physical activity. The family who plays together, stays together, and they will also be healthier, smarter and less aggressive.

The rise of the screen

The IT juggernaut has sent a tsunami of screens—iPads, tablets, smart phones, mp3 players, computers, internet-enabled TVs and game consoles—flooding onto the landscape of childhood and adolescence. It is hard to believe that it was only January 2010 when Steve Jobs launched the iPad! Never before have parents and teachers been confronted with such a sweeping, massive change in human behaviour.

One of the biggest concerns with technology is that it is making our children more sedentary and passive. Another is that you only learn how to be a human from humans. In the early years of life children need to learn how to interact, how to have conversations, how to win and lose, and how to develop friendships. Some children find this much easier to do than others and these children will probably be able to combine their game activities in the virtual world and the interaction in the real world without any problems, with healthy monitoring from their parents. Other children, often our more sensitive children, may struggle to develop the emotional and social competencies to interact in a positive way with other children and adults. My recommendation is to strongly limit preschool aged children with time on technology. Once they get to school, it is very much a part of most learning environments and it can be a great asset in education. When our children use technology as their main source of entertainment and recreational engagement however we need to be concerned.

Keep in mind two key things when making decisions with technology:

1. How much movement and play are my children getting every day?
2. Is the usage no more than the recommended amount for your child's age?

Current government-endorsed recommendations suggest no screens at all for children under two and no more than one hour a day for children two to five. These are great guideposts to what is healthy or otherwise for children under five years of age. Once they have reached all their developmental markers that require movement and real experiences, the influence of technology may be less inhibiting. Over five, the recommendation is to keep recreational screen time to no more than two hours a day.

Signs that screen time may be getting out of balance include:

- tantrums when the child is unable to have technology when they want it (remember it's a privilege that needs to be appreciated, not a right)
- inability to play with other children and have fun
- difficulty sleeping
- more meltdowns and tears over small things—may mean overloaded nervous system

- young children being exposed to games that are not age-appropriate
- poor conversation skills
- poor self-regulation
- difficulty losing when playing with real people
- disconnection to the outside world
- development of a bad habit of neediness—always needing to have a screen nearby
- posture problems.

Throughout early childhood especially, I would still suggest you keep your children as active and as connected to 'real life' rather than the 'virtual life' as possible.

One last sobering message about play comes from Dr Peter Gray, who has written a book called *Free to Learn* (2013). He wrote in a piece for *Aeon* magazine of his concern that lack of play is linked to lack of empathy—which has far-reaching consequences for our society:

> "The decline in opportunity to play has also been accompanied by a decline in empathy and a rise in narcissism, both of which have been assessed since the late 1970s with standard questionnaires given to normative samples of college students. Empathy refers to the ability and tendency to see from another person's point of view and experience what that person experiences. Narcissism refers to inflated self-regard, coupled with a lack of concern for others and an inability to connect emotionally with others. A decline of empathy and a rise in narcissism are exactly what we would expect to see in children who have little opportunity to play socially."
>
> — Peter Gray, *Free to Learn* (2013)

> "Play is the highest expression of human development in childhood, for it alone is the free expression of what is in the child's soul."
>
> — Friedrich Froebel, *The Education of Man* (1885).

Bringing more play into your children's lives

- ☑ Let babies and children direct their own play—everything is interesting!
- ☑ Friendship is shaped by very early connectedness, so give your children lots of opportunities to play with cousins, close family friends and others.
- ☑ Exploratory, undirected play is really important as it stimulates the 'seeking mechanism'.
- ☑ Unstructured play gives children a sense of early autonomy and of having a sense of control in their world—and is vitally important in shaping children's innate character and personality.
- ☑ Cerebellum play—tumbling, spinning, balancing and rolling—enhances the sensory system.
- ☑ Absorbed play is magic—never interrupt a child in this state.
- ☑ Children need more play in the natural world—they can play more creatively, there is better social cohesion, better problem solving, negotiation skills, and deeper immersion in the play experience.
- ☑ Vigorous play helps diffuse excess energy and emotions, and stimulates 'feel-good' chemicals in the body.
- ☑ Games help build emotional competence like learning to lose, to wait your turn, to concentrate and to finish things.
- ☑ The more play the better!
- ☑ The more families play together, the better connected, healthier and stronger they are.
- ☑ Modelling play and sport when children are young gives them a better chance of being healthy and active in life and also helps avoid obesity.
- ☑ Catching and throwing balls with young children helps develop skills that help them achieve well in school.
- ☑ 'Rough and tumble' play with Dad in particular is healthy.

— Maggie Dent, *9 Things* (2014)

Building BLOCK 5

Build life skills

The early years are when children begin to build a toolkit of life skills. As children grow older we simply put more and more life skills into their toolkit. The more tools in the toolkit, the more resilient a child will be. The first tools in a child's toolkit deal with practical things like being able to dress and feed themself, going to the toilet unaided, and being able to play with others. All learning takes time to become solid memory. The development of these early skills will take lots of patience, time and energy by the parent or carer.

> “ All children learn, grow and master life skills at differing rates. There is no competition in raising children.

The life skills toolkit starts from birth, and sometimes the little things, like getting a drink of water when they need to, are the big things. These small milestones build a child's belief in their competence to finish tasks, which in turn helps build their self-esteem. Adults should avoid one or two word commands and talk with your toddlers and young children, saying things like:

- “To be safe we hold hands when we cross busy roads.”
- “Why do we wash our hands after going to the toilet?”
- “Why are vegetables good for us?”
- “What does sour taste like?”
- “Sleep makes our brains and our bodies healthy and smart—so let's get to sleep!”
- “What are seat belts used for?”
- “How do you know when you are thirsty or hungry?”
- “You seem angry that Sam has taken your toy from you—how else can you show your anger without biting Sam?”
- “Shall we clean up all these toys before we have lunch, or shall we do it after we have lunch?”

Conversational language and more coherent speaking opportunities are now seen as equally important as being read to in the first three years of life, for building the pathways to literacy. It allows children to explore conversation and the hidden patterns within the spoken language. It also gives children a sense of being noticed and having value (Kennedy, et al., 2006). This strongly supports the life skill of 'having a voice' and of being heard—attributes of assertive and resilient people. Anyone who feels unheard often struggles with their self-esteem and can feel isolated, unaccepted or undervalued.

Essential life skills include blowing your nose, toileting yourself, using manners, etiquette, road rules, practising good hygiene (such as bathing and cleaning teeth), doing up buttons and tying shoelaces. These are little things that other children may use to tease another child who is not yet competent at them. Parents must be proactive to help their children gain essential life skills so they are able to take care of their needs at an age-appropriate level.

It can also be helpful to help your child learn how to be a good listener before they go to school and also basic organisational skills like putting their coat in their bag. Allowing children to master some of these life skills, especially dressing oneself, can mean there will be times your child will look poorly dressed however the art of 'doing it myself' is incredibly important. They need to be given this golden opportunity and having boots on the wrong feet is a good sign that a child is building competence, not necessarily a sign of poor parenting! Bullying and being teased are very painful and can leave scars that later impact on a person's ability to be resilient.

There are many ways of being intelligent, and one of these ways is emotional intelligence (EQ). Research shows that 80% of a person's potential to be successful in life has to do with their EQ, not their IQ (Goleman, 1996). We must encourage emotional intelligence and competence from the early years because they build resilience.

Qualities of emotional intelligence

- Awareness of feeling states.
- Being able to motivate oneself.
- Persistence in the face of frustration.
- Impulse control.
- Delayed gratification.
- Regulation of one's moods.
- Keeping distress from swamping one's ability to think.
- Ability to accurately empathise.
- Hopefulness.

The main pathways that allow us to understand and manage our emotions are created in early childhood. It has been shown that there are critical time opportunities for young children to develop the ability to be empathetic, gentle and kind. If a very young child is given an opportunity to interact with a small kitten or puppy with adult guidance, they can learn what being gentle and caring means. Children without this opportunity may be unable to care about being rough or hurting others. This inability to feel empathy is a significant behavioural deprivation and could mean that an individual may have difficulty in relationships in years to come, especially when it comes to intimacy. Many children who behave as bullies have problems with empathy. This emotional competency is only learned through life experience and the guidance of a caring adult.

Children will also benefit if they experience a pet dying because this introduces the life challenge of loss. This early education builds resilient responses to recovery, which are needed later in life if they experience a major loss.

Anecdotal evidence suggests that early years' teachers are noticing more children with emotional incompetence. An increased amount of time in front of screens instead of playing in real environments may be a contributing factor. Teachers are finding that some children have poor impulse control and an inability to persist at challenging tasks (Jensen, 2006). Reluctance or refusal to keep trying can impact enormously in the school environment and later in life.

Social awareness has a huge impact on our resilience and is a life skill that takes time to develop—we continue to work on it as adults. Relationships are essential in terms of strengthening resilience when things get tough. Building connectedness is an essential part of the protective factors involved in being resilient.

The strength of humour

In global resilience studies, having a sense of humour is recognised as being a very valuable life skill. It is a huge protective factor in schoolyards where it can protect children from unwanted harassment or bullying. There are so many benefits that can be gained on many levels from laughter.

Laughter:

- transforms emotional states
- stimulates endorphins and creates wellbeing
- increases levels of serotonin
- is a key coping skill, especially for boys
- is an anti-bullying strategy

- encourages lightening up for serious moments
- is a bonding experience when shared in groups
- builds inclusivity and connectedness
- releases tension and stress
- is a key element in effective communication, especially in close relationships
- is an antidote to violence.

Laughter can transform negative emotional states faster than almost any other strategy or technique a parent can use. It is unfortunate that a sense of humour does not arrive in a box underneath the Christmas tree; it would be so much easier than cultivating it as a child has to do, along with so many other life skills.

Death and loss

Coping with significant loss and death is another vital life skill that children can benefit from experiencing while still children. As I wrote earlier, a young child's pet dying introduces the life challenge of loss. The child is able to explore death and to learn that grief creates emotional pain that eventually fades and goes away. They learn about the need to dispose of the deceased's body reverently and that some things bring comfort, like ceremony, prayers, songs or leaving flowers at the grave. This builds a template for future death experiences and builds resilience and the ability to recover, which are needed later in life if and when they experience a major loss.

If you would like to learn more about children and how they process death, please feel free to visit my website (maggiedent.com) and find the "common concerns" page on grief and loss. On there is an article I wrote for *Kindred* magazine called "Death Through the Eyes of a Child", as well as some other resources I have created to support children through grief.

Thinking flexibly

Children who are encouraged to think for themselves are given valuable cognitive processing skills for their whole life. Flexible thinking is definitely a protective factor when adversity hits.

Some resilience researchers (Reivich and Shatte, 2002) even attribute thinking style to be more of a determinant of resilience than genetics, intelligence or any other factor.

Flexible and creative thinking are beneficial in developing real resilience. Children are not little adults. They grow according to their brain and gross motor skill development. They model themselves on significant adults in their lives and are constantly picking up cues from conversations on thinking patterns. Children's thinking skills can be positively influenced by positive adults, and negatively influenced by depressive or aggressive adults.

Solution-seeking kids

An important life skill involves the art of finding solutions. This involves helping children to discover other choices that they could make in response to a challenge, whether a disagreement with a friend or a toy that has broken.

A commitment to search for solutions begins with the adult. Before you fix a problem for a child, help the child to explore ways to overcome it himself or herself. Children do not yet have a frontal lobe in their brains where reasoning and problem solving takes place but they can develop thinking skills that empower them to manage some situations themselves. There is a great temptation for parents to rescue their children from struggles and challenges however this denies them vital opportunities to learn life management skills for themselves.

Children who are surrounded by optimistic language, language that encourages thinking and decision-making, have the opportunity to become resilient when managing setbacks and challenges. They are much less likely to succumb to 'learned helplessness', where they expect adults to always be there to do things for them. There is a line between doing too much for your children and having expectations that are too high, and possibly inappropriate, for your children. Parents need to be careful.

A final note on important life skills is that we continue to face an uncertain future with depleting oil supplies and the effects of global warming. It is more important than ever that we prepare our children by helping them to develop life skills that build on environmental appreciation and ecological sustainability. That might mean making some changes in the way we do things ourselves... certainly food for thought and action.

Parent tips for building life skills

- ☑ **Invest energy throughout your child's early years to help them build basic life skills like dressing themselves, cleaning teeth, toileting, getting own drinks and light snacks, washing hands after going to toilet, tying shoelaces.**

- ☑ As children get older keep adding more and more life skills into the kit bag for life, e.g. cooking, gardening, washing clothes.
- ☑ Engage in simple conversations with your children often—avoid talking at them.
- ☑ Remember that children have to do things many times before the neural pathway is established for learning to occur.
- ☑ Connectedness helps build social and emotional comfort and competence.
- ☑ Ensure that you meaningfully engage with each of your children, especially through repeated play and games—including rough and tumble.
- ☑ Allow children to experience failure and disappointment before offering comfort.
- ☑ Try to get pets that have a habit of dying, like guinea pigs, mice and goldfish so children can experience death and loss.
- ☑ A sense of humour needs to be developed over time. Help your children to learn what is appropriate humour.
- ☑ Be careful to avoid confusing bullying with normal unpleasant events of childhood.
- ☑ Whole communities help children build life skills—everyone can help.
- ☑ Childhood is a time of constant learning. Be careful not to shame a child because he or she is unable to master a life skill.
- ☑ Helping around home by doing regular chores is important for later in life.
- ☑ Take the time to teach skills as children get older—cutting with a sharp knife, cooking, mowing the lawn, painting the house, cleaning the car and definitely how to clean up.
- ☑ Avoid comparing siblings and never assume a child knows how to do something you think they should know.
- ☑ Encourage thinking skills from a young age.
- ☑ Avoid rescuing your children and be careful about doing too much for them.

Building BLOCK 6

Meaningful involvement with positive adults

Being surrounded by safe, caring people helps to build positive expectations for children about their world. Physical, mental and emotional safety is very important. Children are constantly forming perceptions or core concepts that become unconscious beliefs. These deep-seated beliefs become the guiding mental templates from which the child will interpret the world. If a child is ignored or treated with critical words, they are likely to create core beliefs of being 'useless' or 'unlovable' or 'not enough'. For example, a child who struggles with reading in Year One at school may believe that they are dumb and stupid. Readiness to read may occur any time between four and 14 years of age, yet this child's belief system unjustly inhibits them from learning to read. Positive expectations from adults can help a child avoid setting up a self-fulfilling prophecy towards their schooling and all learning.

Most core beliefs are formed before children are seven years of age and shape the way they see the world. Research suggests that negative thought patterns in childhood last for life and can contribute to mental health issues in adulthood, as well as preventing the full realisation of one's potential (Brooks and Goldstein, 2001).

Adults can help children develop positive thought patterns and core beliefs by expressing optimistic language and avoiding shame- and blame-based language. For example, if a child spills a drink a parent could say:

> "Never mind, accidents happen, let's clean it up together."

Or, they could say:

> "How stupid are you? Why don't you watch what you are doing next time?!"

Wired for sensitivity

The separation distress mechanism in the lower brain is genetically wired to be hypersensitive. In the early days of humankind a baby was at great risk if it was separated from its mother; this mechanism ensured that the baby became loudly distressed and so could be found more easily. We must remember that separation hurts babies much like physical pain.

The sensitive early years are a key time for developing core beliefs about trust and safety. Children can be left with other primary carers without any harm, provided the bond of affection is present. The same goes for extended family. If a grandmother dislikes young children and is distant and aloof to them, you could easily be damaging the development of the children's self concepts that they take with them throughout life by leaving them in her care.

I wrote earlier of a condition called learned helplessness. This occurs when a child, often with special needs, receives special care and assistance. After a time, they become dependent on anticipating help and they learn to become helpless. This can happen with over-protective parenting as well, as discussed in the section on building life skills (Reivich and Shatte, 2002). Children only learn life skills by doing them often. This is important for building resilient life patterns that help us overcome adversity and challenge.

Research supports the idea of not hurrying early independence in young children—especially if it is for the convenience of the adults. A clingy, insecure baby needs to be reassured for as long as it takes to grow into a place of new emotional strength. Toddlers whose dependency needs as a baby are accepted and responded to promptly and sensitively, later become the most independent children.

Meaningful involvement can be confused with quality time with a child. Meaningful involvement is an emotional and spiritual connection that can be demonstrated even from a distance. Fathers are vitally important in this circle of love and it is very heartening to see the fathers' movement gaining credibility and synergy in Australia and around the world today.

An aunty or uncle who has a deep connection to a child can show that bond even when living a long way from where the child lives, by staying in touch by phone/Skype. S/he can call and chat about little things as well as the big things, like concerts and other social markers. They may send postcards when they go on holidays and have a special name they call the child that is just between the two of them. They would likely know the child's favourite colour, food and picture books. If the child has a special interest in frogs or bears, they would keep an eye out for articles or posters to get for him or her. This aunty or uncle would come to most if not all birthdays and share in Christmas and Easter family gatherings. This is what meaningful involvement is for a child. The depth of involvement is essential for wellbeing on many levels, especially in later childhood and adolescence. Parents, biological family, non-biological family, child care workers, nannies and even caring neighbours can all fill this need within children. There is only one thing for sure—the more the better, and the deeper the connection the better.

Your presence: the greatest gift of all

The art of 'being present' with a child is an essential building block for a healthy self-esteem. This means being focused on the child and the activity, not thinking of other things or partially focusing on the television or texting/emailing while a child is talking with you. Young children can often detect when you are not being honest.

In a research study done in 1998 by psychologist Raymond Starr of the University of Maryland, he found that abused and neglected children could escape the cycle of becoming abusive parents if they had *one nurturing adult* as their mentor to support them emotionally and psychologically. We can all make a difference in the lives of disadvantaged children. We simply have to have the courage to care and really connect.

How many opportunities are we offering our children so that they can be creative, original and as expressive as they wish? The following list of possibilities has perfect ways for you to be meaningfully involved with your child.

Ponder this:

- Are you comfortable with dirt, mud, paint, water and glue?
- Do you have an area around your home where your child can get 'down-and-dirty' with their creativity?
- Do you have a strategy that helps your child keep his or her creative mess outside, like a cleaning bucket or bowl and towel?
- Do you join in with your child when invited?
- Do you keep the 'creation' as your child leaves it or do you quickly clean it away, as soon as possible?
- When did your child last make a cubby—inside or outside the house?
- Have you brought home any big boxes lately for your child to play with?

- When did you last watch ants or butterflies with your child?
- If your child likes music is it all on a device or do you allow them to make their own sounds and rhythms on pots and pans?
- Do you have screen free days?
- How many sand castles and sculptures have you made?
- How many mud pies have you cooked?
- How many dozen pipe cleaners or popsicle sticks have you bought?
- How many sidewalk chalk packs have you been through?
- What does the outside of your fridge look like?
- Have you ever made capes for your child to wear?
- Have you hand-painted kids' t-shirts with them?
- How many framed kids' 'bits' do you have?
- How many homemade kites have you made and flown?
- When did you last have races with leaf or bark boats?
- When did you last make fresh play dough?
- When did you last have fresh sand in the sandpit?
- How often have you danced with your child?
- Have you made cookies using shape cutters with your child?
- Have you made homemade chocolates in moulds?
- When did you last have a treasure hunt in the garden or park?
- When did you last play hide and seek with your child?
- Have you kept kisses or wishes in a jar?
- Has your child grown anything from seed?
- When did you last take your child to the library to pick out story and picture books they wanted?
- Do you have a box of dress-up clothes?
- When did you take your child camping away from the technological world and into the natural world?

People who are connected to children can also offer some of these possibilities to help tired or busy parents. Respite really helps parents, especially those with challenging, highly spirited children or children with special needs. I have an American friend who always carries small bottles of bubbles for blowing in her handbag for whenever she meets children on her travels. She has made so many special connections with children in trains, planes and shopping centres that she could write a book about it.

Parent tips for creating meaningful involvement

- ☑ Being surrounded by caring, responsive adults is essential for young children.
- ☑ Primary caregivers have a bond of affection for children, for them to feel safe and loved.
- ☑ Meaningful involvement involves trust and unconditional, positive regard.
- ☑ Children need to feel they belong.
- ☑ Being fully present is vital for children of all ages.
- ☑ Solidarity and collective parenting is healthy for families and children.
- ☑ Positive, caring adults can help children learn life skills.
- ☑ The more safe, capable adults in your family circle who can be meaningfully involved, the better for everyone.
- ☑ Volunteer for a school or community mentor program.
- ☑ Be careful to avoid learned helplessness, suppression and indulgence.
- ☑ See every child as a gift or a miracle.
- ☑ We still need a village to raise healthy families.

Building BLOCK 7

Clear boundaries

> “ There is no such thing as a perfect parent or perfect child. Decisions are made according to the circumstance and the current knowledge at the time. There are no ‘one size fits all’ answers.

Healthy, consistent boundaries for children are essential. They need to start from birth and be consistent for each child in a family. When the human brain follows certain rituals or behaviours, it is unstressed and able to focus on the activity. Examples of regular behaviour include always having a bath before or after a child’s dinner and keeping set bedtimes. Children like to anticipate their world and they feel secure when they can predict coming events. Healthy boundaries can reduce stress for children.

There are some key areas where boundaries and routines play an important role in children’s heath and wellbeing and these include:

- sleep
- meal times
- food choices
- manners
- social freedom
- hygiene
- school
- sexualisation (of girls especially)
- screen use—TV/computer/tablets/consoles/Internet
- the ‘I want’ mentality

- childhood versus adolescence versus adulthood
- safety—physical, verbal and emotional
- bullying
- body safety awareness
- homework
- movies, TV shows and DVDs
- overscheduled after school activity.

Sleep deprivation and inconsistent bedtimes impact on learning. The brain needs deep sleep to renew cells and grow new neurons for learning. Good sleep also contributes to better emotional stability and a more agreeable demeanour.

Food choices also require firm boundaries. Adults create the food dynamics of children so it is important that they hold the high ground. It is easy to indulge children for peace, however the peace is short-lived after a sugary treat (see Building Block 2 on nutrition).

At school, children need to behave according to a clear set of rules that ensure everyone's **safety**. Children who have not experienced firm boundaries will struggle in the structured school environment. Often, it is better to stay out of it and leave it up to the school staff and the child to deal with issues around breaking school rules. This will teach them to take responsibility for their own actions, which is important in developing life resilience. Necessary emotional and social development may be delayed if parents intervene inappropriately when their child is being disciplined. Having said that, if the school asks you to assist in reinforcing particular practices/ consequences at home, it can of course be very helpful to work together to support a child's learning.

Boundaries are important around the use of televisions, phones, computers and other devices. When children watch **screens** it means they are not playing and interacting with others (in person) during this time—which is sometimes for up to many hours a day. Immersion in the virtual reality world may create distortions in a child's ability to determine what is real and what is not. The passivity of the activity may also set up patterns of physical lethargy later in life. Allowing children to have screens in their bedrooms creates a pattern of separation from the family. This may create an irreparable gap and make the teenage years more challenging.

Technology and the internet can be problematic for children and parents. Many children are unintentionally exposed to pornographic sites and other inappropriate material, while others have become victims of cyberbullying via emails and mobile phones. See the Building Block on play for recommendations around unhealthy boundaries around screens.

Apply boundaries around **'I want' demands** when your children are young. Instant gratification and indulgence breeds an attitude of neediness to life. This may also lead to an early introduction to the pressures of the consumer-driven world of needing to look like everyone else. Children need to have an understanding that 'no' means no. There are times your children are not meant to like you because you are holding a boundary firm. This is good parenting. You are not meant to be their friend. It can be tricky balancing the mean—needing to be firm and holding your ground around important things—and the loving, being that tender warm and caring parent that every child needs.

> “ Children are meant to be children, looking like children, behaving like children, rather than little adults.

Without boundaries our modern culture can potentially be very damaging and its influence can be insidious and invisible. Parents need to be mindful that our children are not being raised by a media-driven, consumer hungry world rather they are being raised by the adults who created them or who are responsible for their care.

Stand strong because raising children who have a healthy sense of self, with a moral code that respects others and an enthusiasm for making our world a better place takes a lot of time and effort from committed loving parents.

There are no quick fixes to raising children to be decent human beings. No magic pills or potions; it takes time, love and tenderness, and healthy boundaries and guidelines.

Children are quick to forgive, respond even quicker to nurturing love and kindness, and are just a moment away from being magical if we protect them from the shallow and superficial things in life.

Tips for parents on boundaries

- ☑ Boundaries give children predictability and a sense of order in their lives, and reduce the stress that comes from uncertainty.
- ☑ Boundaries build character, and a personal and moral template with which to navigate the world.
- ☑ Parents need to have the courage to be strong and vigilant in maintaining boundaries.
- ☑ Children are meant to be children—especially under 10. Avoid hurrying up your children's childhood.
- ☑ Children spell love T-I-M-E.
- ☑ Create a supportive network of aware parents who will help keep each other's children safe from certain aspects of the modern world.
- ☑ Avoid media that sexualises children or promotes products that have potential for harm.
- ☑ Let the child within you enjoy your children.
- ☑ Be mindful of the 24/7 news cycle, especially around traumatic events and natural disasters. These powerful visual images or audio reports can cause children distress.

Building BLOCK 8

Absence of stress

> "So many grown-ups can't manage stress well. Because no-one helped them enough with stress and distress in childhood, they never set up effective stress regulating systems in their brains."
>
> — Margot Sunderland, *The Science of Parenting* (2007).

Margot Sunderland explores in her excellent book how there are particular ways of responding to children that help them to establish pathways in their brains which enable them to manage emotions well, think rationally under pressure and to calm themselves down without reverting to angry outbursts, attacks of anxiety or, in later life, alcohol, smoking and drugs.

An overactive stress response system originating in childhood can underlie many mental disorders later in life:

- Depression
- Persistent states of anxiety
- Phobias and obsessions
- Physical symptoms and illness
- Being cut off emotionally
- Lethargy and lack of 'get up and go'
- Lack of desire and excitement
- Lack of spontaneity.

— Dent (2014).

Stress is a new challenge to children's health and social wellbeing in our modern world. The hurried and overscheduled child are modern developments. Somewhere over the last 10 years, parenting has become a type of competition—thanks largely to it being more highly scrutinised and idealised in media. The hidden stress this places on growing children causes many other issues that delay healthy development and growth on all levels: emotionally, socially, mentally and cognitively. We have sped up the pace of life and living. We live in an **instant** world where we expect everything NOW. Communication, food, pain relief, results, well-behaved children—you name it, we expect things instantly. This expectation works silently and unconsciously creates stress when things do not happen straight away. We all need to take a breath and slow down for both our children's sakes and our own.

Daniel Goleman (1996) writes, "Happy, calm children learn best". Homes that consciously create calm and quiet times are building enormous support structures that will help children feel safe, allow them to enjoy their own quiet company and lower the stress levels within their growing bodies.

Bruce Lipton in his brilliant book, *The Biology of Belief* (2005), showed that cells in our body can only do one thing—focus on either growth or protection, in order to ensure survival. He says children who live with frequent stress will become sick more often, as their immune systems are suppressed "to conserve energy supplies in order to survive their stressful experience".

Main sources of stress and anxiety in children:

- Hurried, overscheduled world
- Temperaments and personality
- Absence of healthy love and attachment
- Too much pressure on children to perform
- Stressed parents who rush
- Not enough calm, still, quiet solo time
- Poor sleep patterns
- Too much stimulation from TV, hand held devices, toys and adult commands
- Not enough consistency and routines
- Too much social change or social dislocation
- Shaming language
- Threats of abuse and violence
- Death and loss experiences.

Research shows that social dislocation can be highly stressful for individuals. Moving preschools, schools, homes or countries may be a contributor to a delay in some children's intellectual, social and emotional growth. Distress can cause long-term damage to the brain's adaptive systems and these are crucial for resilient behaviour like decision-making, reflection and flexible thinking. Studies clearly link distress with lowered cognitive capacity (Jensen, 2006).

The early years are critical because of the rapid brain growth. The impact of early distress, especially from abandonment, threats or violence, may lead to brain impairment. A child will be more likely to suffer from depression, stress and anxiety disorders, and a lower IQ.

Setting boundaries and being consistent carers with similar expectations of how to behave helps reduce stress for toddlers and children. It is very confusing for children when they receive different instructions and discipline. Stress is a response to the perception of lack of control. Children are susceptible to stress because they seldom have much control over their environment.

> "An essential component of resilience and high self-esteem is the belief that one has some control over what is occurring in one's life."
>
> — Robert Brooks and Sam Goldstein, *Raising Resilient Children* (2001).

The opposite of stress and distress is calmness and feeling relaxed. If a child clings to you, s/he is trying to bring down a high body arousal level and high levels of stress chemicals. S/he is trying to activate the positive brain chemicals that activate feelings of wellbeing. Research shows that children who have been soothed quickly and frequently, tend to become self-soothers and manage stress better (Sunderland, 2007). Due to the neuroplasticity of the human brain, calmness can be learned at any stage of life.

Top tips for soothing: Key ways to trigger oxytocin—the love neurotransmitter

1. Calm adults with calm voices
2. Touch and massage—especially 'tickle point' (high on back, along shoulder base—stroke gently)
3. Rocking
4. Sucking
5. Physical comforters—soft toys, dummies, blankets

6. Warmth, approx 21 degrees C—(or cooling if child has a temperature)
7. Low soothing sounds, familiar songs or white noise
8. Bathing in warm bath
9. Novelty—laughter
10. Avoid overstimulation, especially loud voices, noises, too much chaos, and too much change.

Older children can be taught calming strategies and relaxation at any time. I cover this extensively in my book, *Saving Our Children from our Chaotic World: Teaching Children the Magic of Silence and Stillness* (2003).

Avoiding too many rules is also important as they create a 'police state'. Ensure that the rules set are easy to remember and follow, and that everyone in the family knows them. Identify five key guidelines that work well, and as they grow older you may need to add new ones to the list. Always use calm voices and do not threaten when you are trying to create a stress-free environment. Allowing plenty of spaces for child-directed activities helps children to feel in control of their world.

Quietness, silence and stillness are important in children's lives. There needs to be times when there is no noise, no specific activity and a space from the business of their daily lives. These quiet times allow the brain to come 'offline' to sort and process new learning and to explore how things fit together in their minds. Memory and thinking are both enhanced with quietness.

Moments of calmness allow children to experience the state of 'absorbed play', where they become so absorbed by what they are doing that they lose track of time. This is an experience of 'oneness' within themselves and a total absence of stress. This quiet place within is valuable later in life when experiencing adversity. It helps us understand how to navigate our way out of challenges, and access our inner wisdom, not just the cognitive, rational mind.

Creating moments of joy and delight with music and smell is really important for young children because it also sets up calming pathways in their minds. When my boys were ill with a fever I would hum a lullaby or sing to them and it really helped them to settle. Recent research on the power of lullabies confirms that they soothe upset babies; apparently the number one lullaby is *Twinkle Twinkle Little Star*. Relaxation audio tracks with music and calming voices have the same effect and evoke feelings of safety and calmness.

Safe touch is also incredibly important in all human relationships. If we consider a traditional kinship community, where the circle of women were constantly in close proximity to all the children, the ability to get a hug or a cuddle whenever you needed would have been really easy.

> "Many of the infant and child behaviours that are challenging parents in our culture are unheard of in cultures that practise high-touch nurturing. Babies are biologically programmed to expect the same high-touch nurturing that evolved millions of years ago."
>
> — Pam Leo, 'Connection Parenting' in *Kindred Magazine* (June-August 2008).

Tips to calm your home

- Remove clutter and mess because it can add to a child's perception of being in chaos and out of control.
- Play music that soothes the brain—anything from classical to nature sounds.
- Ensure boundaries are clear and healthy around meals, sleep, siblings and safety.
- Take children out into the fresh air as often as possible.
- Use calming aromatherapies.
- Practise small acts of kindness and generosity.
- Use quiet voices and ask politely rather than demanding.
- Really listen to your children—without interrupting.
- Use safe touch through foot or back massages.
- Use life-enhancing language that encourages a positive mindset.
- On a nightly basis use calming, creative visualisations for everyone.
- Stimulate more play and creativity.
- Have a teddy bears' picnic purely for fun.
- Ensure parents take care of themselves.

Children depend on parents and other significant carers to help them develop healthy stress-regulating systems so they can manage stress and anxiety.

The more love and affection, calm surroundings, safe nurturing touch, and predictable routines the better chance children have of growing the neural wiring that will allow them to be happy and psychologically strong for life. So start, now—take three deep breaths and relax.

> “Our world continues to be a place of conflict and uncertainty. It will continue to be so while we seek out the differences between people, cultures and countries. There is no one right way of living or being. With mindfulness and calmness we are so much more likely to use compassion and kindness in our interactions with everyone else. Maybe if we searched for the sameness within others there would be more harmony.”
>
> — Maggie Dent, *9 Things* (2014).

There is a Buddhist saying that goes something like this:

> When there is peace in the heart, there will be peace in the home, there will be peace in the country and there will be peace in the world.

Parent tips for reducing stress in children

- ☑ Children benefit from calm quiet spaces in their world.
- ☑ Avoid being rushed and hurried.
- ☑ Use quiet voices with gentle tones.
- ☑ Have regular quiet times in your home when electronic stuff is shut off.
- ☑ Allow children time just ‘to be’ and not always be busy.
- ☑ Children sense their parents’ stress and react to it—so reduce your stress.
- ☑ Ensure children have good night sleep patterns.
- ☑ Calmness can be learned—do a relaxation activity with them.
- ☑ Avoid too much noise and visual stimulation in homes.
- ☑ Avoid too much exposure to TVs, computers, smart phones and other electronic games and devices.
- ☑ Create safe home environments with boundaries and routines.
- ☑ Avoid too much significant change in children’s lives.
- ☑ Avoid pressuring your children.
- ☑ Soothing and reassuring children triggers oxytocin and calms children.

Building BLOCK 9

Self-mastery

Self-mastery is the natural progression from the absence of stress. Achievement and success builds an authentic sense of self-esteem and self-value. Even being able to do up buttons is self-mastery. Life is a continual journey of self-discovery, growth and the realisation of more of our human potential. Children need to have others to help them become competent and taste success so they can take it into adulthood.

It is important for parents and carers to provide many varied physical and mental activities for their children to experience before they start school. School presents the opportunity to learn new skills, and children who have had positive, interactive early childhoods tend to learn better. Basic literacy is very important in developing resilience because the ability to read and write increases the chances of life success. We need a basic level of literacy to read road maps, emails, SMS, fill in application forms and other documents or contracts.

Learning and achievement is improved with practice, and parents play a vital role in supporting children in those formative years. Sometimes kicking a football, catching a ball, shooting netball goals or searching for rare frogs in the dark are what parents need to do to help their child become competent at something. Conquering a new boundary like swimming faster, playing a recognisable tune on a piano, being able to bake a cake, or ride a bike without training wheels is essential in building a healthy sense of self. It teaches a key element of resilience—"I am capable."

No one person is excellent at everything. With the understanding of multiple intelligences we now recognise that we have innate abilities and talents, and ones that we need to work on.

Mastery can happen in small ways for children—sometimes almost unnoticed—and parents can never quite tell when they have mastered something. One day they may be able to drink easily out of a cup, and the next day spill it everywhere. Remaining encouraging and supportive is helpful, especially when they struggle to master a new skill like sharing toys or falling asleep easily.

Many people have etched into their minds the day they rode their bicycles without training wheels. One grandmother came up to me once and said how amazing it was when a child mastered riding a bike without training wheels. The night before her 14-year-old grandson with cerebral palsy had phoned very excited to tell Nan that he could finally ride his bike without training wheels. She said she cried with joy for his new mastery. The taste of sweet success becomes a healthy motivator for children to learn; they have also learned that mistakes can be corrected and overcome with persistence. These are very important emotional competences that children develop when they are young. Overcoming setbacks is a critical part of resilience.

> “ Few children have learned to ride their bicycles without a few skinned shins or knees. This is valuable, real learning for children who learn to understand that we can recover and overcome setbacks.

Real experience means that rather than telling children about vegetables and that they are grown in the ground, we create a patch or a tub and plant something with them. Children who have been taken to lots of interesting places learn so much faster and more comprehensively than those who have not. Allowing children opportunities to milk a cow, collect manure and pick strawberries creates lasting learning and shapes the way they see the world.

Young children develop in different ways and at different times, and parents and teachers need to be careful not to force developmental boundaries by urging children to master tasks prematurely. This is happening in some preschools where early childhood teachers are being asked to get children to take early reader books home. There are significant developmental parameters that must be respected or you may unintentionally teach a child they are a failure or dumb because they are not ready to tackle that task. Competence develops confidence and, unfortunately, the reverse is true as well. Despite the curriculum-driven focus of much of the world's early years' education, children respond to the world in their own unique way, in their own time, and when they are in a safe and caring environment.

> "Learning and success encompass so much more than getting ten out of ten for a spelling test. Learning and success are about inner happiness, intrinsic motivation and having the confidence and competence for discovery and learning."
>
> — Kathy Walker, *What's the Hurry?* (2005).

Small acts of self-mastery are just as important for children as the big ones, like making a sandwich or doing a handstand. This building block links back to life skills—the more things a child can do for themselves, the more confident they feel in their ability to tackle new things.

Self-mastery is not just for kids; a vital part of adults' growth is learning to have humility when things we thought we had mastered go awry. This is something that allows children to feel safe; the capacity to allow vulnerability to appear as a normal part of meaningful relationships. My challenge to eat spaghetti bolognaise without having some drop on my generous bosom is something I am yet to master—this lack of ability has been the source of great mirth and delight within our family, and will continue to be so forever. Our children do not need for us to be perfect, just real and to able to own life's little moments when they appear as they are, not as they could be.

Parent tips for building self-mastery

- ☑ Every child ever born has their own unique gifts and talents—every child is different.
- ☑ Multiple intelligences mean we have different ways of being smart.
- ☑ Find special interests when children are young and encourage these interests.
- ☑ Developing an internal locus of control is healthy. External ones like being competitive, the thinnest or thinking that problems are always someone else's fault will result in personal challenge.
- ☑ Being able to express oneself and be heard are important in growing in self-mastery.
- ☑ Allowing children to experience failure, and conflict helps them to develop strategies to overcome the same later in life.
- ☑ Life-enhancing language will help children keep attempting a task until they master it.

- ☑ Small things are the big things—buttons, shoelaces, blowing noses successfully, mastering knives and forks, cleaning teeth, blowing bubbles, riding bikes, and climbing trees.
- ☑ Helping children grow in mastery takes lots of patience, time and many, many repeated attempts because children's brains are unable to comprehend what the adult brain can, and the plasticity of the brain takes time to wire new learning.
- ☑ Seeking and encouraging unique strengths in each sibling is important.
- ☑ Doing works better than telling, lecturing or nagging.
- ☑ Being enthusiastic without being overly pushy with children's accomplishments is tricky.
- ☑ Having high, positive expectations for our children is important without having unrealistic ones (especially ones we may not have fulfilled when we were children).
- ☑ As children get older, mastery in real tasks like doing regular chores, cleaning shoes, making lunches, fixing things with Mum or Dad, cooking, washing the car, attending to small cuts and grazes, addressing letters, painting and even changing light bulbs helps children feel confident and competent. There is a window from 5–9 years of age where they love to help and by adolescence the novelty seems to leave.
- ☑ Encourage an awareness and respect of the environment and the natural world.
- ☑ Teach children how to make healthy snacks.
- ☑ Teach children some basic first aid.
- ☑ Teach children road rules when walking or riding a bike.
- ☑ Learn to comfort without paralysing—encourage and acknowledge more than you praise.

Building BLOCK 10

Strengthen the spirit

> "The body of a child will not grow if it is not fed; the mind will not flourish unless it is stimulated and guided. And the spirit will suffer if it is not nurtured."
>
> — Rachael Kessler, *The Soul of Education* (2000).

We have both emotional and spiritual competencies that help us build resilience. People who have overcome huge adversity will often identify a moment in time when they felt strengthened by something deep within them, rather than just a rational thought.

The stronger the human spirit, the less disconnected and separated we feel within the world. Just as we have IQ and EQ I believe we have SQ—Spiritual Quotient.

Spiritual intelligence

- Wonder
- Respect and reverence
- Awe
- Relational spirituality
- Lightness and laughter
- Contemplation
- Calmness, stillness and quiet
- Tenderness and gratitude
- Simplicity
- Listening with the heart.

— Maggie Dent, *Nurturing Kids' Hearts and Souls* (2005).

Children need to experience the joy of discovery—feeling rain for the first time, touching a kitten, or seeing Christmas lights. The moment of awe must be experienced while young for it to be a powerful part of adult life. These experiences of heightened sensation allow children to feel transcendent—somehow more expanded and larger than life. The search for transcendence can drive later experiences. Those who have had positive natural 'highs' as young children are more likely to seek natural thrills rather than seek them through drugs or high-risk activities as they become teenagers and adults.

> "The most beautiful thing we can experience is the mysterious. Recognition of the mystery of the universe is the source of all true science. He to whom emotions are a stranger, who can no longer pause to wonder and stand rapt in awe is as good as dead; his eyes are closed."
>
> — Albert Einstein

Happy children have a strong spirit and know that life is full of anticipation, delight and fun. The more of these experiences children have up to 10 years of age the better. The brain wires all positive experiences like a web over all future experiences and builds a sense of anticipation of how life will be. Children who have had moments of sheer fun and enjoyment will tend to anticipate and expect more of those moments as an adult.

The imaginary world of children is an essential part of strengthening their spirit. Plenty of experiences that include fairy tales, tooth fairies and imaginary friends build a healthy base for a strong spirit and creative mind. These are helpful for building resilient adults.

Laughter needs to be experienced often so that it becomes an easy part of life and we can learn to reframe negative experiences into lighter moments. Chemical changes happen in the brain that help us diffuse stress, improve our emotional state and allow us to review the situation from a more optimistic place (Goleman, 1996). Encourage young children to tell jokes and riddles, and to laugh lots.

The natural world helps strengthen the human spirit whether it is a beautiful garden, a park, mountain or the beach. The open spaces and fresh air automatically release stress and then energise in a healthy and nourishing way.

To avoid chaos in the house, try taking your family for a walk or to play in the park. A healthy respect and connection to the natural world is a part of all resilient people.

The human spirit is strengthened by loving relationships in which there is genuine positive regard and acceptance. Acts of kindness towards others always build our own spirit and sense of value.

> "Human connectedness is the key to resilience, authentic happiness and a sense of wellbeing. This can only be achieved through the recognition, honouring and nurturing of the human spirit that exists within every child ever born."
>
> — Maggie Dent, *Saving Our Children from Our Chaotic World* (2003)

Parent tips for strengthening the spirit

- ☑ Children need to experience the joy of discovery.
- ☑ The human spirit is strengthened by loving relationships.
- ☑ Have special home and classroom rituals that show everyone matters.
- ☑ Work at building strong caring relationships—no matter how hard it may be.
- ☑ Feeling loved and valued is essential to a strong spirit.
- ☑ Allow imagination and wonder to be a part of children's lives.
- ☑ Develop an appreciation of cultural diversity—all peoples are more alike than different.
- ☑ Ensure the arts are part of every day—singing, dancing, music, painting, make-believe and storytelling.
- ☑ Laughter and lightness nurture the spirit.
- ☑ Connection to nature is very important for the growth of the whole child.
- ☑ Hope is a powerful force—without it there is nothing but profound fear, emptiness and despair.
- ☑ Acts of kindness towards others always builds our own spirit and sense of value.
- ☑ Strengthening communities from the grass roots is essential in building children's resilience and wellbeing.
- ☑ Remember the little things are sometimes the big things for toddlers and children.
- ☑ For children, the gift of the imagination is a powerful source of comfort, distraction and escape.
- ☑ A strong spirit will help individuals overcome setbacks and adversity.

Building them up BLOCK BY BLOCK

Communities that protect the families within their boundaries play an enormous role in the healthy raising of children. When a child's needs are at risk, the community must step up and be there for as long as is needed.

It is time to recognise that governments have limited success at a community level because the grassroots reality means that without trust and respect, money is simply money and cannot solve our problems. The synergy that is needed must come from within each community—it is a community of people with courage and a passionate humanity that holds the light of hope. There is nothing quite like the power of hope and we must never give up on our children.

> "Real kids need slow childhoods that allow them to grow on all levels—mind, body, heart and soul. They need deep connectedness with living things like people and pets to grow in their capacity to build nurturing, loving relationships later in life. This is what we all yearn for and seek and real kids who have been able to be real kids have the best chance at achieving it."
>
> — Maggie Dent, *Real Kids in an Unreal World* (2008).

I hope the information contained within these pages supports parents to make decisions that will help them to raise children who are happy, healthy, strong, kind and resilient. Not perfect children but rather children who will find a way to use their unique gifts and talents in some way to make our world a better place.

I especially hope that we give permission to our kids to be kids, and that we give them the gift of a childhood with noise, chaos, unpredictability, mess, unbridled excitement, squealing joy and peak moments of mastery!

Let there be laughter, let there be lingering, let there be love as our little precious beings that we have created, or agreed to care for, walk this amazing journey of life. May they know that they have come here to be themselves, not some version of our reality or of our story of who they should be. Let us gather circles of support that build human connectedness, which truly honour the value of family within communities.

RECOMMENDED READING

Daniel Siegel and Tina Payne Bryson, *The Whole-Brain Child: 12 Revolutionary Strategies to Nurture Your Child's Developing Mind, Survive Everyday Parenting Struggles, and Help Your Family Thrive.* (2011).

Rachel Macy Stafford, *Hands Free Mama: A Guide to Putting Down the Phone, Burning the To-Do List, and Letting Go of Perfection to Grasp What Really Matters!* (2014) and *Hands Free Life: Nine Habits for Overcoming Distraction, Living Better, and Loving More* (2015).

Justin Coulson, *What your child needs from you: Creating a connected family* (2012).

Shelley Davidow, *Raising Stress-Proof Kids: Parenting today's children in tomorrow's world.* (2014)

Steve Biddulph's *Raising Boys* (4th ed.) and *Raising Girls* (2013).

Laura Markham. *Peaceful Parent, Happy Kids: How to Stop Yelling and Start Connecting* (2012).

John Medina, *Brain rules for baby: How to raise a smart and happy child from zero to five* (2010).

Janet Lansbury, *Elevating Child Care: A Guide to Respectful Parenting* (2014) and *No Bad Kids: Toddler Discipline Without Shame* (2014).

BIBLIOGRAPHY

Biddulph, S., & Biddulph, S. (2001). *Love, Laughter and Parenting in the Years from Birth to Six.* St Leonards, NSW: Dorling Kindersley.

Brooks, R. and Goldstein, S. (2001). *Raising Resilient Children.* New York: McGraw Hill.

Dent, M. (2014). *9 Things: A back-to-basics guide to calm, common-sense, connected parenting birth-8.* Murwillumbah, NSW: Pennington Publications

Dent, M. (2005). *Nurturing Kids' Hearts and Souls: Building emotional, social and spiritual competence.* Dunsborough. WA: Pennington Publications.

Dent, M. (2008). *Real Kids in an Unreal World. How to build resilience and self esteem in today's children.* Dunsborough, WA: Pennington Publications.

Dent, M. (2003). *Saving Our Children from Our Chaotic World: Teaching children the magic of silence and stillness.* Dunsborough, WA: Pennington Publications.

Dwyer, N. (2013). *Being Adventurous: An everyday learning series title.* Deakin, ACT: Early Childhood Australia. Available from www.earlychildhoodaustralia.org.au/shop/details.cfm?prodid=984

Estroff Marano, H. (2008). *A Nation of Wimps: The high cost of invasive parenting.* New York: Broadway Books.

Froebel, F. (1885). T*he Education of Man.* New York: A. Lovell & Company.

Gerber, Magda. *The RIE Manual For Parents And Professionals.* Los Angeles, CA: Resources for Infant Educarers, 1979.

Gill, T. (2007). *No Fear: Growing up in a risk averse society.* UK: Calouste Gulbenkian Foundation.

Goleman, D. (1996). *Emotional Intelligence: Why it can matter more than IQ.* UK: Bloomsbury Publishing.

Gonzalez-Mena, J. & Widmeyer Eyer, D. (2008). *Infants, Toddlers and Caregivers: The Philosophy of Respect based on the work by Magda Gerber and the Hungarian paediatrician Emmi Pikler.* New York: McGraw-Hill.

Gray, P. (2013) *Free to Learn: Why Unleashing the Instinct to Play Will Make Our Children Happier, More Self-Reliant, and Better Students for Life.* New York: Basic Books

Gray, P. (2013, September). The play deficit. *Aeon.* Retrieved 3 October 2013 from www.aeonmagazine.com/being-human/children-today-are- suffering-a-severe-deficit-of-play/. This article was originally published in Aeon Magazine: www.aeon.co

Grille, R. (2013). *Parenting for a Peaceful World* (second edition). Asheville, NC: Vox Cordis Press.

Jackson King, J. (2010). *Raising the Best Possible Child: How to navigate parenting myths and bring up confident, happy kids.* Australia: HarperCollins.

Jensen, E. (2006). *Enriching the Brain.* San Francisco, CA: Jossey-Bass.

Kennedy, A., Ridgway, A. and Surman, L. (2006). *Boundary Crossing: Negotiating understandings of early literacy and numeracy. Australian Journal of Early Childhood.* December. Monash University.

Kessler, R. (2000). *The Soul of Education: Helping students find connection, compassion and character at school.* USA: ASCD Publications.

Landy, J., & Brown, A., PhD. (2008). *Kids with More Zip: A practical guide for educators/carers focusing on long term health and movement experiences for children ages 3 to 12.* Nedlands, WA: Allan Borushek Family Health Publications.

Lipton, B. H. (2005). *The Biology of Belief: Unleashing the power of consciousness, matter and miracles.* Santa Rosa, CA: Mountain of Love/Elite Books.

Neufeld, G., & Maté, G. (2005). *Hold On To Your Kids: Why parents need to matter more than peers.* New York: Ballantine Books.

Pearce, Joseph Chilton. (2002). *The Biology of Transcendence: A blueprint of the human spirit.* USA: Park Street Press.

Peterson C., Maier, S.F. and Seligman M.E.P. (1995). *Learned Helplessness: A theory for the age of personal control.* New York: Hoeber.

Reivich, K. and Shatte, A. (2002). *The Resilience Factor.* New York: Broadway Books.

Sunderland, M. (2007). *The Science of Parenting: How today's brain research can help you raise happy, emotionally balanced children.* New York: DK Publishing.

Walker, K. (2005). *What's the Hurry?: Reclaiming childhood in an overscheduled world.* Australia: Australian Scholarship Group.

Whitebread, D., Basilio, M., Kuvalja, M., & Verma, M. (2012). The *importance of play: A report on the value of children's play with a series of policy recommendations.* Written for Toy Industries of Europe (TIE). Retrieved October 6, 2013 from www.importanceofplay.eu/IMG/pdf/dr_david_whitebread_ the_importance_of_play.pdf

ABOUT THE AUTHOR

Commonly known as Australia's 'queen of common sense', Maggie Dent is an author, educator, and parenting and resilience specialist with a particular interest in the early years and adolescence. Maggie was a teacher for 17 years before working as a counsellor with young people and their families, in suicide prevention and in palliative care and the funeral industry.

Maggie is an advocate for the healthy, common-sense raising of children in order to strengthen families and communities. She is a passionate, positive voice for children of all ages.

Now an in-demand writer and speaker, Maggie is a regular contributor to Fairfax's Essential Kids website, *Parenting Ideas* and *Teachers Matter* magazines, on commercial and ABC radio around Australia, and on TV programs such as The Daily Edition, Sunrise, Today and news.

She is the author of eight books, and a prolific creator of resources for parents, adolescents, teachers and early childhood educators.

Maggie is the proud mother of four sons, and an enthusiastic and grateful grandmother.

www.maggiedent.com
Facebook, YouTube, Soundcloud: /maggiedentauthor
Twitter: @queenofcommonse
Instagram: maggiedentauthor

OTHER RESILIENCE RESOURCES FROM MAGGIE DENT:

MORE PARENTING BOOKS FROM MAGGIE DENT